"*The Stress Relief Journal* is a friendly and empowering aid for anyone who wishes to do more to help themselves. By inviting the reader to use their natural mindfulness to notice and record their present-moment experience while engaging in a variety of mind-body practices, the authors have provided an accessible, helpful, and transformative path into the realm of mindful awareness and mind-body healing."

—**Jeffrey Brantley, MD**, emeritus professor in the department of psychiatry at Duke Medical Center, founder of the Mindfulness Based Stress Reduction program at Duke Integrative Medicine, and coauthor of 5 *Good Minutes of Mindfulness*

"This is a book that should be on every adult's reading list and handed out to every child in school. Let's face it, the world is a stressful place, and we all need to learn to relax. This book will show you how with a fun, easy-to-use journal."

—**Jeffrey C. Wood, PsD**, coauthor of *The Dialectical Behavior Therapy Skills Workbook* and *The New Happiness*

"*The Stress Relief Guided Journal* provides research-backed tools in an approachable and user-friendly tone. Actively managing stress has huge health and mental health benefits, and this journal is an easy way to get started."

—**Elena Welsh, PhD**, author of *5-Minute Stress Relief* and *The Panic Deck*

"*The Stress Relief Guided Journal* provides readers with a plethora of fast and effective stress management strategies, and is sure to become a go-to source for those wanting to improve self-awareness and reduce stress. Whether you're a mental health professional working with clients, or someone looking to quickly regulate your stress response, this workbook will be a valuable resource for years to come."

—**Jennifer Sweeton, PsyD**, clinical psychologist, and author of four books on trauma treatment

"Stress affects every single human—that's why this handy journal needs to find its way into everyone's hands! The authors do a terrific job of putting together exercises that can be done in five-minute sit-downs, so that our self-help doesn't add more to our plate. This book will definitely find its way to my recommendation shelf for clients!"

—**Katie Krimer, MA, LCSW**, psychotherapist at Union Square Practice, self-growth coach at Moxie, and author of *The Sh\*t I Say to Myself*

"*The Stress-Relief Guided Journal* is an inspirational, easily digestible guide to reducing your stress. It focuses on your body, mind, and emotions using well-researched techniques like breathing and muscle relaxation, and innovative strategies based on mental imagery and hypnosis. It is written in a clear, positive, and simple style, and can help you understand the different facets of your stress and give you concrete stress-relief skills. I highly recommend it."

—**Melanie Greenberg, PhD**, author of *The Stress-Proof Brain*, clinical psychologist specializing in stress and trauma, and international trainer and speaker

"Stress and pain are nearly unavoidable in our daily lives; to be human is to be stressed. Learning to manage stress is a key life skill to avoid hours of frustration, self-criticism, and inaction. This guide shows readers a wide range of micro-skills to permanently change the way you handle stress."

—**Patricia E. Zurita Ona, PsyD**, director of the East Bay Behavior Therapy Center, and author of *Living Beyond OCD Using Acceptance and Commitment Therapy* and *Acceptance and Commitment Skills for Perfectionism and High-Achieving Behaviors*

# New Harbinger Journals for Change

Research shows that journaling has a universally positive effect on mental health. But in the midst of life's difficulties—such as stress, anxiety, depression, relationship problems, parenting challenges, or even obsessive or negative thoughts—where do you begin? New Harbinger *Journals for Change* combine evidence-based psychology with proven-effective guided journaling techniques to help you make lasting personal change—one page at a time. Written by renowned mental health and wellness experts, *Journals for Change* provide a creative and safe space to process difficult emotions, work through challenges, reflect on what matters, and set intentions for the future.

Since 1973, New Harbinger has published practical, user-friendly self-help books and workbooks to help readers make positive change. Our *Journals for Change* offer the same powerfully effective tools—without ever *feeling* like therapy. If you're committed to improving your mental health, these easy-to-use guided journals can help you take small, actionable steps toward lasting well-being.

**For a complete list of journals in our *Journals for Change* series, visit newharbinger.com.**

# The Stress Relief

## GUIDED JOURNAL

### Your Space to Let Go of Tension and Relax in 5 Minutes a Day

Matthew McKay, PhD | Patrick Fanning

New Harbinger Publications, Inc.

NEW HARBINGER PUBLICATIONS is a registered trademark of New Harbinger Publications, Inc.

New Harbinger Publications is an employee-owned company.

Copyright © 2023 by Matthew McKay and Patrick Fanning
New Harbinger Publications, Inc.
5674 Shattuck Avenue
Oakland, CA 94609
www.newharbinger.com

All Rights Reserved

Cover and interior design by Amy Shoup

Acquired by Ryan Buresh

Edited by Joyce Wu

Library of Congress Cataloging-in-Publication Data on file

Printed in the United States of America

25    24    23

10    9    8    7    6    5    4    3    2    1              First Printing

# Table of Contents

# Introduction

**This is a simple journal with only one purpose**—to help you relax. Open to any page and you'll find the space you need to slow down, to explore your stress and your responses to it, and a relaxation technique that you can learn in five minutes.

For each journal entry you'll find open-ended space to reflect on the stress in your life and a way to practice relaxing. The journal is based on the growing body of research that proves the benefits of journaling. Whether you are an avid journaler or this is your first time, we bet you intuitively know that a daily writing practice helps to give you much-needed "you time"—a space to explore your inner world, notice parts of your day, and reflect on what it means to be a person in the world. This journal takes that intention and applies it to understanding the stress you are experiencing on a deep level.

The daily relaxers in this book have been distilled from the best and most effective techniques that therapists have been using for decades. These "best of the best" relaxers have been proven to reduce your physical tension, calm your mind, refresh your spirit, and relieve painful feelings such as anxiety and depression. When you are able to relax at will, you feel better, look better, sleep better, like yourself better, and get along better with those around you.

This journal is easy to use. You don't have to use it all. You don't have to use it in any particular order. Browse until you find an appealing technique. But we do recommend that in order to get the most out of it, you commit to using it every day.

There's enough in here to keep you learning new ways to relax for a while, but we predict that in just a few weeks, you'll find yourself returning to some favorite techniques that fit your personality and circumstances best. That's fine. Work your habits into your daily routine and practice them for as long as you enjoy them. If you eventually get bored with the same two or three relaxation methods, don't worry. Repetition and practice are essential. Think about how often stress interrupts our lives—to get the maximum benefit we need to process the stress as a habit and way of living. If a certain practice in this book gets stale, try another idea and explore new depths of yourself.

If stress overwhelms you and you forget how to relax, don't be discouraged. Everybody struggles with stress. Just remember that tomorrow is a new day and a new chance to make relaxation part of a permanent lifestyle of stress reduction.

"Your body is always talking

to you. Its voice is loudest

when it needs to relax."

# PART I:

# Explore Your Stress Response

# ••• BODY CHECK-IN •••

Take three deep breaths and rate your stress level:

$$1 \quad 2 \quad 3 \quad 4 \quad 5$$

How relaxed are you at this moment in time?

_____

_____

Where is the tension in your body?

_____

_____

Your body can actually tell you more about relaxation than any book can. It knows volumes about your unique states of tension and release. All you have to do is turn your attention within and quietly listen.

What is your body telling you that you need in this moment?

_____

_____

_____

_____

Remember to thank your body for keeping you alive and informed, for serving you even when you've ignored its needs. **Write a quick note of gratitude to your body, despite any tension you're feeling:**

_____

_____

_____

One time today, pause in a quiet spot and close your eyes. Allow your breathing to slow and deepen. Ask your body, "Where are you tense?" Scan your body for any tight neck or back muscles, sore joints, tiny aches and pains in your arms or legs, little twitches around your eyes, or places where you are hunched up to protect tender spots. **Note them here:**

_____

_____

_____

**Tell your body, "It's okay—we don't need this tension or this soreness anymore. We can let it go."**

•   •   •

Do something special for your body today: take a bubble bath, get a manicure, use some hand lotion, or wear your most comfortable clothes.

Keep checking in with your body. It will tell you truths you need to know, secrets you cannot hear from any other source.

# Take Your Stress Temperature

**Take a few deep breaths.** Where is the tension in your body?

_____

_____

_____

_____

_____

_____

_____

_____

One of the surest signs of illness is when your temperature gets too high. It's an adaptive strategy to help you fight infection, but it's also an outward sign that is hard to ignore. Stress also sends physical messages through our bodies, but despite that, it sometimes can get ignored.

Take a moment and consider your stress right now. Circle how high you think your stress is on the scale to the right.

10
9
8
7
6
5
4
3
2
1
0

Now take a second to list any physical symptoms you have been having lately. Think of things like a tired jaw from clenching, being more fatigued, difficulty remembering. List any symptoms below:

_____

_____

_____

_____

_____

What might be influencing your stress temperature at this moment?

_____

_____

_____

_____

_____

_____

How often do you feel like your stress temperature is high? Can you find any patterns?

_____

_____

_____

_____

_____

_____

_____

When your stress temperature is high, what are some ways you typically try to deal with it?

_____

_____

_____

_____

_____

_____

If your stress temperature is still high now, brainstorm three things you could do right now to lower it. That could be taking a moment to slowly stretch or move your body. Pampering yourself in some way. Getting an extra hour of sleep if that feels right. Choose one and try it.

**1**

_____

_____

**2**

_____

_____

**3**

_____

_____

_____

# Stress Family Tree

**Take a moment to reflect** on some of your tried-and-true remedies for finding relaxation in the face of stress. List them below:

1. _____

2. _____

3. _____

4. _____

5. _____

6. _____

7. _____

8. _____

9. _____

10. _____

Think back to your childhood—was there anyone, maybe a parent or other family member, that you saw or remember using one of the same strategies you just listed? Maybe there is more than one person. Why do you think they might have used that stress coping strategy? How do you think it worked for them?

Coming back to the present, how do your stress strategies work for you?

If you could change one thing about how you handle stress, what would it be?

# Your Stress Alarm

**Stress and tension can build up quietly** until your stress alarm goes off at the least opportune moment. It can feel like suddenly a fire alarm is blaring and you're completely overwhelmed by stress.

Take a few deep breaths. Then try to remember a moment when your stress alarm went off. What did it feel like?

_____

_____

_____

_____

_____

_____

Looking back on that moment, what might have triggered it?

_____

_____

_____

Think about when your stress and tension set off alarm bells. What signs did you miss that your stress was building?

_____

_____

_____

_____

_____

_____

If you could go back in time, before your stress alarm starting ringing, and give yourself one piece of advice, what would it be?

_____

_____

_____

_____

_____

# Describe Your Stress Habits

**Find a comfortable position and take five deep belly breaths.** How are you feeling in this moment?

_____

_____

_____

_____

What might be contributing to how your mind feels?

_____

_____

_____

_____

_____

_____

_____

When you think about your stress levels over time, what are some things that might commonly affect how stressed you feel?

_____

_____

_____

_____

_____

_____

_____

_____

_____

_____

_____

Whether you know what sorts of things commonly stress you out or it's a mystery, you can learn a lot about your stress by simply tracking it.

Over the next week, track how your habits hurt or help your stress. Record three instances of stress and your daily habits to get a sense of how your habits hurt or help your stress.

**1**

Date: _____ Hours of sleep the night before: _____

Situation/Events: _____
_____
_____
_____

How you felt: _____
_____
_____

What you ate during the day: _____
_____
_____
_____

What physical activity did you engage in during the day: _____
_____
_____

Date: _____ Hours of sleep the night before: _____

Situation/Events: _____

_____

_____

_____

How you felt: _____

_____

_____

What you ate during the day: _____

_____

_____

_____

_____

What physical activity did you engage in during the day: _____

_____

_____

Date: _____ Hours of sleep the night before: _____

Situation/Events: _____

_____

_____

_____

_____

How you felt: _____

_____

_____

What you ate during the day: _____

_____

_____

_____

_____

What physical activity did you engage in during the day: _____

_____

_____

Over the last week, what patterns did you notice? Was there any connection between how you felt and things like your diet, exercise, or sleep? Write down whatever you noticed:

Now that you've tracked your stress for a week, is there any habit you want to add or improve on? Why might it be a good idea to focus on that habit?

# Your Stress Response

**Think back to a moment when you suddenly felt stressed out.** Describe that time below:

As your stress alarm was blaring, what did you do to try to lower your stress?

_____

_____

_____

_____

_____

_____

Looking back on your stress relief method, how did you feel an hour later?

_____

_____

_____

_____

_____

What about a day later?

What would a perfect stress response strategy look like for you?

Without judgment, are there any other strategies you could try to respond to your stress?

_____

_____

_____

_____

_____

_____

_____

Let's commit to trying something new the next time you feel stressed.

## The next time I am stressed out, I will:

_____

_____

_____

_____

_____

_____

# The Stress-Less Pledge

**So you've picked up this guided journal** because you are committed to trying to get a handle on your stress. You have made the first step. In the space below, take time to write out a pledge to yourself about this commitment. Why are you doing this? What do you hope to gain? What would it feel like to lower your stress level? How will you respond to setbacks and challenges along the way?

_____

_____

_____

_____

_____

_____

_____

_____

_____

_____

You can find a blank copy of this and other free tools at
New Harbinger's website for this book: http://www.newharbinger.com/51673.

# • • • Stress Relief Check-In Moment • • •

Take three deep breaths and rate your stress level:

( 1 )    ( 2 )    ( 3 )    ( 4 )    ( 5 )

Where is the tension in your body?

_____

_____

_____

What might be impacting your stress levels today, negatively or positively?
Explore below:

_____

_____

_____

_____

_____

_____

How do you feel about the stress in your life? Is it high? Doable? Why did you feel that you needed this journal in this moment?

How far away does relaxation feel at this moment in time?

How has your stress level been affected by working through this journal so far?

How does your stress level compare to one week ago?

"One of the

first steps toward

true relaxation must start

with your body."

# PART 2

# Let Go of Tension

# Paying Attention

**Paying attention to a problem will sometimes solve it.** Tension in your body is a problem that you can start to fix by just paying more attention. When you feel tense or nervous, try simply noticing your physical sensations. Take a moment to write down what you notice now even if you have little to no tension:

_____

_____

_____

_____

_____

_____

_____

_____

Of course, it's difficult to remember in the middle of rush hour or an exam that you're supposed to notice and list your physical sensations. In those situations, you're usually oblivious to your bodily state, but taking a moment to do this quick attention practice can help you refocus on your body. We recommend you practice and get a sense of it now or in a moment when you aren't super stressed out.

- Sit in a comfortable position and close your eyes.

- Take several deep breaths.

- Bend your right arm at your elbow, out to the side, and lift the arm so that the tips of your fingers are about even with the top of your head. In other words, raise your hand as though you want to ask a question. Hold it in this position for a while.

- As your right arm begins to tire, focus on the sensation of tiredness.

- Scan your body and see if other muscles are tightening. Take several deep breaths and gently say to your muscles, "Relax," or "Let go."

- After three or four minutes, lower your right arm slowly until it rests in your lap. As you lower it, use the following prompts to focus on the sensations.

Which muscles or parts of your arm were strained and which were not?

Can you identify the moment at which the muscles that held up the arm relaxed? How did your discomfort grow or change? Does it go away as soon as the arm moves? Does it go away gradually?

_____

_____

_____

_____

_____

_____

Is there any discomfort as your arm rests on your lap? Can you still feel the muscles you were so aware of when your arm was raised?

_____

_____

_____

_____

# Out with the New, In with the Old

**Being able to recognize the difference** between relaxation and muscle tension—often so chronic it goes unnoticed—is a key skill.

Find a comfortable position. Take a few deep breaths. Scan your body for tension. What do you notice about how your body is feeling?

_____

_____

_____

_____

Is there anything recent, like an injury or an odd sleeping position, that may be causing you tension? What is contributing to how your body is feeling?

_____

_____

_____

_____

# Progressive Muscle Relaxation

Let's have you try an exercise called **Progressive Muscle Relaxation** in which you tighten each muscle group, then release.

- Take a deep breath, way down into your abdomen. As you exhale, let your whole body begin to relax.

- Curl both fists, tightening forearms, biceps, and pectoral muscles (Charles Atlas pose). Hold for seven seconds and relax.

- Notice the *feeling* of relaxation in your arms and chest.

- Wrinkle up your forehead. Hold for seven seconds and relax. At the same time, roll your head clockwise in a complete circle.

- Then reverse it. Notice the *feeling* of relaxation in your forehead.

- Now make your face like a walnut: simultaneously frown, squint your eyes, pinch your lips, and hunch your shoulders. Hold it for seven seconds and relax.

- Notice how it *feels* when your face and shoulders deeply relax.

- Gently arch your back and take a deep breath into your chest.

- Hold the position, as well as your breath, and relax.

Take another deep breath, this time pressing your stomach out. Really let it bulge. Hold for seven seconds and relax. Again, notice how it *feels* to relax your back and stomach.

Now flex your feet and toes. Tighten your buttocks, thigh, and calf muscles. Hold for seven seconds and relax.

Last, point your toes out (ballerina style) while again tightening your buttocks, thighs, and calves. Relax after seven seconds. Notice what your legs feel like when they really relax.

Briefly scan your body and allow yourself to feel the relaxation spread from head to toe.

Notice the *feelings* of relaxation in your body. What does it feel like?

_____

_____

_____

_____

_____

_____

Brainstorm how you might be able to incorporate this exercise into your daily routine:

_____

_____

_____

_____

_____

_____

_____

_____

_____

_____

_____

_____

# Where Is Here? When Is Now?

**One of the key principles of finding calm** in the heart of a stressful episode is simple: stay rooted in the here and now. Buddhist teachers compare the mind to a restless monkey, always darting off to grasp something new, something *not* here and now. If you spend a lot of time obsessing about the past, worrying about the future, or wishing you were someplace else, that's your "monkey mind" at work. You can tame the monkey by consciously focusing on the here and now.

Using this journal, sit quietly and ask yourself: *Where is here?* Be as descriptive as possible. Look at everything around you. What are the smells and sounds?

And now ask yourself, *When is now?* Close your eyes for a moment and visualize the room you are in. Some of the things you see will bring up memories or future plans. When this happens, tell your monkey mind, *That's not here right now.* Then return to exploring the here and now.

---
---
---
---
---
---
---
---
---
---

The next time you feel stressed by a busy schedule or frustrated aspirations, take a moment to ask yourself, *Where is here? When is now?*

# The Breath of Life

**Breath is a necessity of life.** Each breath you take is a small miracle of chemistry and physics. Take a moment to pay grateful attention to the breath of life.

Next time you are feeling stressed, try noticing your breathing. Describe it to yourself—is it shallow and quick, or deep and slow?

How are you feeling in this moment?

How has your stress level been over the last week or so?

Try this breath-counting technique to help you relax:

- Set a timer for five minutes.

- Lie down on your back and raise your knees a little.

- You can close your eyes or just gaze at the ceiling in an unfocused way.

- **Take slow, deep breaths into your stomach.** Don't strain to overfill your lungs—just make them comfortably full.

- **Pay attention to each part of the breath:** the inhale, the turn (the point at which you stop inhaling and start exhaling), the exhale, the pause between breaths, and so on.

- **When you've developed a smooth rhythm, begin counting your breaths.** As you exhale, say, *One.* Continue counting on each exhalation up to four.

- **Then begin again with one.** You may become so relaxed that your mind wanders and you lose track. When this happens, start over with one.

Reflect on how you feel after the exercise. What did your thoughts turn to? What did you notice about your breath?

# Instant Relaxer

**When two unrelated events occur at the same time** (for example, a chime rings every noon while a monk is saying his prayers), the events become linked in the mind. Eventually, if they occur together often enough, one event can trigger feelings and reactions associated with the other (the mere sound of the noon chime can stimulate the peace the monk feels from praying).

Smells and sounds are really good for this. Take a second to think of something that triggers a specific memory. What is it and what is the memory? Describe it in detail:

_____

_____

_____

_____

_____

_____

_____

_____

Now, what feelings does this memory bring up?

_____

_____

_____

_____

_____

_____

_____

_____

_____

Now choose a cue word or phrase that will become linked to feelings of deep relaxation. With a little practice, the mere thought of your cue word, like what signals fond memories, will trigger a simultaneous muscle release throughout your entire body.

The first step is to choose your cue word or phrase. Make it something that pleases you, but it also helps if the cue phrase tells you exactly what to do. You might even choose a favorite color or place as your cue word. Anything will work as long as it is linked, through practice, to feelings of relaxation.

Here are some examples:

- *Relax and let go*

- *Breathe and release*

- _____

- _____

- _____

- _____

The second step is to relax using the same sequence of muscle groups that you learned for Progressive Muscle Relaxation—but this time don't tighten anything. Just relax each muscle group.

- ⬤ Take a deep breath. Say or write your cue phrase.

_____

_____

_____

- ⬤ Relax your forearms, biceps, and pectoral muscles.
- ⬤ Take a deep breath. Say or write your cue phrase.

_____

_____

_____

● Relax your forehead. Take a deep breath. Say or write your cue
  phrase.

_____

_____

_____

● Relax your eyes, cheeks, lips, jaw, neck, and shoulders. Take a deep
  breath. Say or write your cue phrase.

_____

_____

_____

● Relax your back and chest. Take a deep breath. Say or write your cue
  phrase.

_____

_____

_____

● Briefly scan your body for any remaining tension. How do you feel?

_____

_____

_____

The point of practicing is to turn your cue into something that immediately conjures feelings of relaxation. To progress your practice, you relax all muscle groups *simultaneously*, while taking a deep breath and thinking of your cue phrase. Focus on muscles that need to relax and empty them of tension. Try practicing this first when things are quiet and peaceful. Then begin using your cue phrase in slightly tense situations at home or work. Brainstorm an upcoming situation in which it might be good to use this practice:

Keep practicing until you can cue relaxation even while your boss looks steamed or your children are fighting in the backseat. And remember, as with any technique, you must invest the time to master this skill. It works!

# Visualizing Relaxing Metaphors

**What metaphors do you habitually use** when you think or talk about stress? Do you describe your cold hands as ice blocks or your headache as pounding? Do you think of your sore muscles as tied up in knots?

How does it feel to think of your stress that way? What might be some unintended consequences of your metaphors?

_____

_____

_____

_____

_____

_____

_____

_____

_____

_____

_____

Metaphors are powerful—they can literally create feelings. Just as a stress metaphor might increase tension, you can use metaphorical images of relaxation to visualize tension away.

For example, a hot color, like red, could represent tension, and you would change it to a more relaxing color, like blue or green.

Here are some metaphorical images you can use for quick relaxation visualization:

- *Screeching chalk on a blackboard crumbling into powder*
- *A screaming siren fading to the whisper of a flute*

Try writing your own relaxation metaphor:

_____

_____

_____

_____

_____

_____

_____

_____

Try expanding on your metaphor as much as possible. Really use your imagination. Form mental sense impressions involving all your senses: sight, hearing, smell, touch, and taste. For instance, imagine the sights of a green forest with the trees, blue sky, and white clouds overhead, and pine needles underfoot. Then add the sounds of wind in the trees, babbling brooks, and birdsong. Include the smell of pine, the taste of mountain spring water, and the feel of the warm sun or the ground under your shoes.

The next time you feel stressed, you can reread your metaphor or simply close your eyes, lie down, and visualize your metaphor.

Write down a short version of your metaphor to bring to mind as a mantra of sorts when you don't have much time:

# Autogenic Breathing

**Imagine that your arms and legs are getting warmer**—as if, for example, you were lying in the sun. Use the space below to describe an environment in which you might feel warm. Let your mind travel to the warm beach, where the weight of the sand gently pressing on your arms and legs calms you and relaxes every muscle in your body. Be as detailed as possible.

Now, if you didn't already, imagine you're at the beach. You can see the seagulls wheeling overhead and you can hear their calls. The waves are rolling up the sand. The surf roars and then grows quiet, rushing in and then receding. Let yourself be lulled by the roar...quiet...roar of the waves.

Keep describing this in detail. Keep breathing.

Continue to breathe deeply, finding the relaxation in every breath. Notice the rhythm of your breathing. And as you breathe in, think the word *warm*. Really concentrate on feeling the warm sand around your body. As you breathe out, think the word *heavy*. Focus on the weight of the sand on your arms and legs.

Continue your deep breathing, thinking *warm* as you inhale and *heavy* as you exhale.

How do you feel now?

# Relaxing Your Blood Pressure

**As you've learned in the last few sections,** the human imagination, expressed in simple imagery and affirmations, is very powerful. Did you know your imagination can lower your blood pressure?

Think of familiar things that operate under pressure, such as car tires, air compressors, carbonated beverages, or water nozzles. Imagine pushing in the little valve stem on a car tire and letting out some of the air pressure.

Compose a very short phrase to go along with your image of releasing pressure. Put three or four words together that sound right to you.

_____

_____

_____

_____

_____

Start at your ankles and work your way up your body from joint to joint: knees, hips, lower back, shoulders, elbows, wrists, and finally neck. At each joint, visualize your image of reducing pressure and recite your phrase.

Try writing down the phrase and placing it somewhere you see often. Or try adding a phone reminder that pings the phrase to you throughout the day.

# Today's Gift of Pleasure

**Take a moment to notice** or remember something small and beautiful you experienced today. Describe it in as much detail as you can:

There should always be time to appreciate the gifts of life. But sometimes it's hard to stop and smell the flowers, isn't it? Especially when it feels like there aren't enough minutes and hours in the day to accomplish everything that must be done. Why do you think that is?

Try making a promise to yourself right now to take just half a minute today to notice and enjoy something simple in your daily path. Write down what it looks like to commit to a simple practice of pleasure:

Brainstorm ways you could try organizing your day so you can keep all those moments from flying away.

You could also try this technique if you often make to-do lists. The next time you make a things-to-do list for your day, imagine that you have a desk with three drawers. On top of the desk is the space for all the things that are going to make you feel good today. Just below that, in the top drawer of your desk, put all the jobs that simply must be done today. In the middle drawer, put all the things that are pretty important, but not as urgent as the top-drawer items. In the bottom drawer, put all the stuff that you'd like to get to, but the world wouldn't end if you had to put them off until tomorrow. Use this structure to organize your day.

On Top of
the Desk:


Top Drawer:


Middle Drawer:


Bottom Drawer:

Shut the bottom and middle drawers and don't open them until the jobs in the top drawer are done. No cheating! Then do *all* the middle drawer items before moving on to the bottom drawer.

However far you get today, you can rest assured that you have worked on the most important jobs. Here's a hint: most of the things in the bottom drawer won't be missed if you don't ever get to them.

At the end of the day, congratulate yourself and reorganize your drawers for tomorrow. And take a moment to write out your experience of anything today that felt good and gave you pleasure:

_____

_____

_____

_____

_____

_____

_____

# • • • Stress Relief Check-In Moment • • •

Take three deep breaths and rate your stress level:

( 1 )   ( 2 )   ( 3 )   ( 4 )   ( 5 )

Where is the tension in your body?

_____

_____

_____

What might be impacting your stress levels today, negatively or positively?
Explore below:

_____

_____

_____

_____

_____

_____

How do you feel about the stress of your life? Is it high? Doable? Why did you feel that you needed this journal in this moment?

_____

_____

_____

How far away does relaxation feel at this moment in time?

_____

_____

_____

How has your stress level been affected by working through this journal so far?

_____

_____

_____

How does your stress level compare to one week ago?

_____

_____

_____

"You must learn to live in the moment

by surrendering your anxious thoughts

to moments of peaceful reflection

and rhythmic breathing."

# PART 3

# Calm Your
# Frazzled Mind

# Moving Band Meditation

**So far, you have focused a lot on the physical tension** you've been feeling because of stress. But as you know, stress can leave our minds frazzled, burned out, and spinning. Thinking about your experience of stress, how could you describe your mental state when you are stressed?

What thoughts do you have?

What is your mind often asking for in times of stress?

When your mind is racing, it can be effective to do a classic moving band meditation because it turns your attention inward and narrows your focus to immediate sensations.

- Get into a comfortable sitting position and take a deep abdominal breath.

- Imagine that a three-inch-wide band encircles the top of your head.

- Try to bring your full attention to the area of your head that's covered by the imaginary band.

- Be aware of any physical sensations in your forehead. If you notice tension, see if you can release it.

- Lower the imaginary band three inches, so that it covers your nose and mouth. Focus your full attention on the area under the band.

- Take a deep breath as you say to yourself, *Let it go, let it all go.*

- Just continue to move the band down your body, lowering it three inches at a time (the width of the band). Be aware of all sensations, particularly any tension. As you release the tension, take a deep breath and remind yourself to *let it go.*

- When the band reaches your feet, let it snap open and disappear. Imagine your whole body emanating a pale blue light. You are deeply relaxed, completely at peace.

How did that meditation make you feel?

What is one thing you can do for your mental health today? Something to give your mind a break?

# Special Place

**You likely picked up this book** because you need a place where you can escape, where you can be protected from pressure and stress for a while.

Reflect on the last place you have been—it can be a vacation or a room—where you felt safe and relaxed. Picture it in your mind and describe it:

_____

_____

_____

_____

_____

_____

_____

_____

_____

If this place is real and nearby, you might go there when you're overwhelmed, but sometimes there is no such refuge or it is inaccessible. That's when you need to create a safe and peaceful place in your imagination, a place you can go any time you need to relax. Let's create it now. Your safe place can be real or fictional. Close your eyes and focus on the image of your special place.

Describe how it looks, smells, feels, and sounds:

_____

_____

_____

_____

_____

_____

_____

_____

You can use your special place visualization at your desk at work, just after parking your car, for a moment when your kids are playing with their toys, or any time you can close your eyes for thirty seconds and take a slow breath, way down into your abdomen. Feel your whole body becoming heavy and calm. See what's around you, hear what's around you, feel what's around you—explore it.

If you like, you can practice shuttling back and forth between your special place and your real environment.

Start with your eyes closed for thirty seconds in your special place, then open your eyes and use the journal to describe your actual surroundings:

_____

_____

_____

Close your eyes for thirty more seconds in your special place, then describe your actual surroundings again, and so on, for five or six complete cycles. If you practice in this way, shuttling back and forth will get you to a point where you can enter your special place almost instantly. From then on, it can be a relaxing haven whenever and wherever you need it.

My special place is _____

Where I am now is _____

_____

_____

_____

_____

_____

_____

_____

# Withdraw into Blackness

**It may surprise you** that a lot of stress enters through your eyes. Bright sun or car headlights make you squint. Clashing colors can make you irritable. Long hours of reading make your eyes sore.

Tired eyes seek blackness as a rest from vigilance and the daily image assault. Blackness shuts you off from the real world and forces you to "look in" on yourself—a physical impossibility and a spiritual necessity.

Try enjoying blackness a couple of times a day. It just takes a minute. Seated at a desk or table, ask yourself, *What am I seeing now?*

Put the heels of your palms directly over your closed eyes. Block out all light without putting too much pressure on your eyelids. Try to see the color black. You may see other colors or images, but focus on the color black.

Return to the page and write a few permissions for yourself about how you are allowed to feel in the dark. Focus on release of tension or permissions to do nothing for a minute. Be creative. Tell yourself you don't have to look at anything right now.

_____

_____

_____

_____

_____

_____

_____

Now go back into the darkness. Let the muscles around your eyes relax—your eyelids, under your eyes, the crease between your brows, your forehead, your cheeks.

After a minute, slowly lower your hands and gently open your eyes. Remind yourself throughout the day that at almost any moment, you can close your eyes and escape into blackness.

# Pencil Drop

**When your high-pressure lifestyle** meets a low ebb in your energy level, together they can stir up an emotional whirlwind that makes everything you value—your loved ones, your work, your hopes and dreams—seem like debris swirling around you.

Have you ever felt this way? What was it like? How did you feel? How did you act?

Mentally, what kind of thoughts did you have?

Read the following to yourself out loud:

"I am the calm center of the whirlwind. I can take a moment to right myself, to return to center. At my core is a calm spot that does not turn with every gust of wind."

How does it feel to say this aloud? Describe the feeling or try drawing yourself with a calm center:

Your calm center is always available. If you ever lose sense of it:

- Pick up a pencil by the point end. Hold it very lightly between your thumb and fingertip, letting the eraser end hang down a couple of inches above the tabletop.

- Cradle your head in your other hand and get as comfortable as you can.

- Close your eyes and consciously slow your breathing.

- Tell yourself that when you are sufficiently relaxed, the pencil will slip out of your fingers and drop. That will be your sign to let go completely, to just relax and feel peaceful for two minutes.

- Imagine the description or picture you drew of yourself with a calm center.

- After the pencil drops, continue to enjoy your calm center for a couple of minutes. Then return to what you were doing with renewed energy—feeling calm, relaxed, and focused.

# Gazing at Special Things

**Find a special stone, ring, shell, or other small object** you've collected and retained. Find a nice place to sit, free from a lot of distraction. Take a few moments to sit and look at it.

Use the space below to describe it:

_____

_____

_____

_____

_____

_____

_____

_____

_____

_____

Or, if you are more of a drawing person, try sketching it:

Now change your position relative to your special object. Place it roughly at eye level, about a foot away from you. Set a timer for ten minutes.

Look at this special thing carefully. Gaze rather than stare at it. Keep your facial muscles relaxed—don't frown or squint at the object.

Without using words, engage with the object—try to feel with your eyes its softness or roughness, the sharpness or dullness of its angles, its weight and density. Words and thoughts about the use or meaning of the object will surface in your mind. That's fine. Just notice them and let them go.

Let yourself become totally immersed in the experience of exploring this object, as if you have never seen it before and it is the most fascinating thing in the universe.

Take a moment to reflect on how you now feel:

_____

_____

_____

_____

_____

_____

Take a moment to reflect on what this object means to you:

_____

_____

_____

_____

_____

_____

_____

_____

What does the object remind you of? Is there a special time you associate with the object? What was that like?

_____

_____

_____

_____

_____

_____

_____

_____

_____

_____

_____

_____

Has your stress level changed?    **YES**  or  **NO**

What was it about that memory that may be helping you feel less stressed?

_____

_____

_____

_____

_____

_____

_____

What's one key relaxation nugget you can take from either your special object or the memory and associations it brought up for you?

For the rest of my day, I can _____

_____

_____

_____

_____

# Changing Colors

**Visualizations that use strong, evocative colors** often produce a powerful effect.

- Set a timer for ten minutes.

- Take a deep, slow breath. As you continue to breathe deeply, close your eyes. Scan your body from head to toe.

- Now visualize your body as a map or a dark silhouette, lit from the inside by dozens of red (tension) or blue (relaxed) lights.

- Where do you feel any tension or red lights? Circle them on the body outline.

- Where do you feel any blue lights? Circle those places, too.

What do you think is causing your red lights?

_____

_____

_____

_____

_____

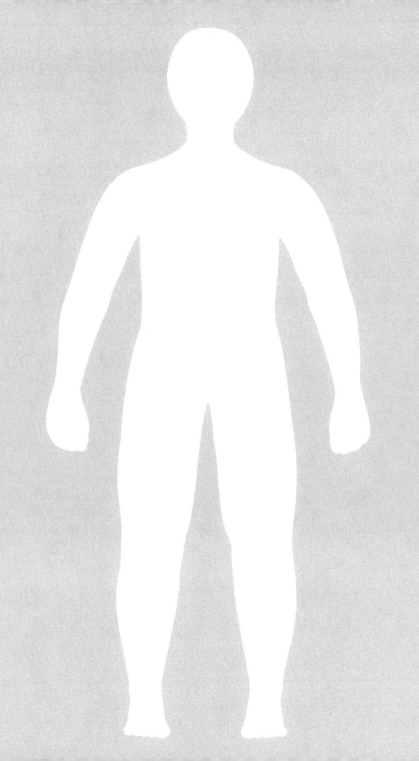

While continuing your deep breathing, imagine the lights turning from red to blue in all the tension areas of your body. Feel yourself growing calmer as the red lights dim and disappear one by one. When the map of your body glows completely blue, experience the peaceful feeling of release.

To deepen the relaxation, imagine the blue lights glowing a lighter and lighter hue; let them slowly connect up until your whole body is suffused with a calming white or blue-white light.

Take a moment to reflect on how it would feel for you to be made of nothing but calm blue light:

_____

_____

_____

_____

_____

_____

What is something you can do today to decrease the amount of tension you feel?

_____

_____

# Going Deeper and Deeper

**When was the last time you zoned out** or felt a little hypnotized by something? What was it like? How did you feel?

_____

_____

_____

_____

_____

_____

_____

_____

_____

_____

_____

_____

You've already been hypnotized many times without knowing it, going into a trance state while driving or daydreaming. Even trying to remember a shopping list or lounging in front of the TV can induce a temporary hypnotic state. You may also have been in a shock-induced trance following a scary experience.

Your mind has the capacity to disconnect from the pain and pressures of the moment. Hypnosis can offer you a vacation from stress while it refocuses your mind on healing and relaxing imagery.

Before trying the following induction, you'll need to do two things in preparation. First, brainstorm how you could create an image of a safe and peaceful place. It should be a place that's comfortable and calm, and beyond the reach of anything stressful or threatening. Describe the place here (or go back to the Special Place exercise and use what you wrote there).

Second, develop one or two suggestions that will help you stay relaxed when you come back to the real world. Make suggestions for the immediate future (so your subconscious has time to put them into practice). The following list might give you some ideas:

- *I can awake refreshed and rested.*

- *My body is feeling more and more healthy and strong.*

- *My mind will remain cool and relaxed throughout the day.*

- *Whenever I start to worry, I can take a deep breath and let go.*

You give it a try:

- ●  ------------------------------------------------------------

  ------------------------------------------------------------

- ●  ------------------------------------------------------------

  ------------------------------------------------------------

- ●  ------------------------------------------------------------

  ------------------------------------------------------------

- ●  ------------------------------------------------------------

  ------------------------------------------------------------

- ●  ------------------------------------------------------------

  ------------------------------------------------------------

- Start by closing your eyes and taking a slow, deep breath. Take a second deep breath and focus on relaxing your body as you exhale.

- Draw a staircase leading down to your special place.

- Now close your eyes, but keep the image of the staircase in your mind.

- Count each step going down to your special place, and with each step you will become more and more deeply relaxed.

- Count slowly backward from ten to zero.

- Each number you count is a step going down.

- Imagine that saying each number and taking each step helps you feel more and more deeply relaxed. You can count backward from ten to zero once, twice, or even three times.

- At each complete count, say your phrase...

- When you're ready to come out of your trance, imagine climbing back up the stairs. In between numbers, remind yourself that you are becoming "more and more alert, refreshed, and wide awake." As you reach number nine, tell yourself that your eyes are opening; at ten suggest that you are totally alert and wide awake.

Our suggestion is to try recording this on your phone—that way you can hear your own voice talking you in and out of hypnosis.

When would be a good time to schedule a self-hypnosis session?

After the session, reflect on your experience:

# Doorway of Release

**Have you ever spent a whole day going over worrisome thoughts**—stewing and simmering emotionally and mentally over whether you should do this or do that, debating if you should call that person or not call, wondering whether to follow your instinct or resist it?

Use the space below to describe these moments and to release them onto the page:

Do you often find yourself returning to similar mental loops? What are the contents of those loops?

Visualize yourself
standing alone in a
corner of an empty,
white room. Describe
or draw yourself below:

There are no distractions—no television, no phone, no furniture, no clutter of material objects of any kind. You feel safe in this room, but you are aware of pressing thoughts swirling about you; your mind is filled only with your worries and concerns.

Now draw doors in your room. Both doors open into space or into an empty void of darkness. You are watching your thoughts spiral in from one of the doors. There is no need to either hold on to or to resist these ponderings.

Now take a few moments to identify and write these worries as they arrive:

_____

_____

_____

_____

_____

_____

_____

_____

_____

After you've labeled five or ten of your most pressing thoughts, imagine these thoughts leaving through the other door and twirling into outer space. Thoughts come in and thoughts go out. Watch them, label them, and then let them go.

Take a few worry thoughts from your list and use them to complete the following sentences:

I am letting go of the thought _____

_____.

I am letting go of the thought _____

_____.

I am letting go of the thought _____

_____.

I am letting go of the thought _____

_____.

Remember that you can return to this quiet room for release whenever you feel stuck in a dead-end loop of distressing thoughts.

As a worry thought enters the room, you can always open a door and release it.

## "I am relaxed, I am at peace."

# Your Coping Monologue

**A coping monologue is a series of positive affirmations** you prepare before you have an interview, exam, date, or other stressful situation.

Strange as it sounds, you actually choose and intensify your emotional reactions to any event by your predictions, interpretations, and self-evaluations. To see how this works, think about a moment you dreaded. It could be something coming up in the future too.

The event: _____

What did you predict would happen?

_____

_____

_____

_____

_____

_____

_____

_____

Were there any signs you looked for to assess how this dreaded event was going?

What things did you notice about yourself in that moment? Did you feel nervous? Did you feel like someone else could see how you felt internally?

And how did your body feel? Were you sweating or did you have a knot in your stomach?

_____

_____

_____

_____

_____

_____

_____

_____

_____

_____

_____

_____

Noticing these physical reactions, you may have thought, _I'm panicking. I can't do this. I've got to go home._ These self-statements increase your physical symptoms and your tendency to make poor decisions. A negative feedback loop is formed and you spiral into a state of chronic stress.

Your thoughts can also flip the script. You can prepare a coping monologue to act as a tranquilizer for a tense stomach, calming you and pushing away panic. The feedback loop can be a positive one, working for you instead of against you.

When you have a stressful appointment coming up, write down positive self-statements to help you prepare for the situation, confront it, cope with your fear, and reinforce your success. Here are some examples:

| Write yourself a preparation statement: | I've got nothing to worry about. <br><br> Everything will be all right. <br><br> I've done this before. |
| --- | --- |
| confrontation: | Just go step by step. <br><br> It's okay to make a mistake. <br><br> I can do this—I am doing it. |
| coping with fear: | Keep breathing deeply. <br><br> It will be over soon. <br><br> I've survived worse situations than this before. |
| reinforcing success: | I did it! <br><br> I coped with my fear and succeeded. <br><br> I've got to tell somebody about this. |

Now you try:

| | |
|---|---|
| **Write yourself a preparation statement:** | |
| confrontation: | |
| coping with fear: | |
| reinforcing success: | |

It helps to write down your favorites on an index card and take the card with you to the performance evaluation, audition, interview, or whatever situation is going to make you nervous.

# Make a Chill Habit

**To understand conscious living,** you have to start by asking, "How do you relax when you aren't relaxing?" How do you relax if you have to walk six blocks to the store, or drive home on a busy freeway, or wash a pile of dishes after dinner? The answer is to do things with *awareness*—to experience fully the act of walking, driving, or dishwashing.

In order to relax, you need to focus your mind on the same task your muscles and senses are engaged in. You can learn to harmonize your senses, muscles, and mind when doing simple everyday tasks such as walking, driving, or washing dishes.

## WALKING

How would you describe your walking habit now?

_____

_____

_____

_____

_____

_____

Now try this:

- Walk a little slower than your usual pace, noticing your breath.

- Say to yourself, *In*, with each inhale, and *Out*, with each exhale.

- While continuing to label your breath "in" and "out," try to time your walking so that you start to inhale or exhale at the precise moment one of your feet hits the ground.

- Get used to this for a few minutes, saying *in* and *out* while getting your steps in sync with your breathing.

- Now add one more thing. Count your steps while breathing. Say to yourself, *In, two, three, four, out, two, three, four*. Or the count might be, *In, two, three, out, two, three*, if you're walking slower.

- Just maintain awareness of your breath and the act of walking, keeping as accurate a count as you can.

Describe your experience with mindful walking:

_____

_____

_____

_____

_____

_____

# DRIVING

How would you describe your driving now? Try to describe as many of the details as possible:

Conscious driving requires complete focus on the road.

So, the first step is to get rid of distractions: turn off the radio, don't drink or smoke, and put away that half-eaten donut. Now give your *full* attention to the act of driving. Be aware of these things:

- Your distance from the car in front of you
- Your speed relative to other cars or the speed limit
- The positions of cars to the side, and cars that are oncoming
- The condition of the road
- The weather and other driving conditions

Now comes the hard part—keeping your senses, mind, and muscles in harmony. When any thought enters your mind that isn't related to the act of driving, let it pass and gently return your focus to the road. Many thoughts will try to intrude, but you can push them away each time. Try this meditation for three minutes or so at a time.

How was it when you tried this?

_____

_____

_____

_____

_____

_____

_____

_____

_____

## DISHWASHING

How do you feel about doing dishes right now?

_____

_____

_____

_____

_____

The key to conscious dishwashing is to focus your full attention on the experience of washing a dish. Try to notice the following:

- The warmth of the water
- The sensation of wetness on your hands
- The hard and slippery surface of the dish
- The pressure and effort of scrubbing, the crusts of food dissolving away
- The smooth feel of dish soap, and the feel of soap bubbles
- The act of rinsing away all evidence of soap

Try to keep your mind from wandering from this moment, this experience. Really try to focus on the sensations.

How was the experience?

# • • • Stress Relief Check-In Moment • • •

Take three deep breaths and rate your stress level:

$1$   $2$   $3$   $4$   $5$

Where is the tension in your body?

_____

_____

_____

What might be impacting your stress levels today, negatively or positively?
Explore below:

_____

_____

_____

_____

_____

How do you feel about the stress of your life? Is it high? Doable? Why did you feel that you needed this journal in this moment?

_____

_____

_____

How far away does relaxation feel at this moment in time?

_____

_____

_____

How has your stress level been affected by working through this journal so far?

_____

_____

_____

How does your stress level compare to one week ago?

_____

_____

_____

"When we stop and listen to the

voice of our spiritual selves, it

always guides us to a place of

peace and belonging."

# PART 4

# Refill Your Cup

# Letting Go

**Worries and troubling thoughts** can take on a life of their own. Troubling thoughts make you feel more anxious, sad, or ashamed, which in turn triggers more troubling thoughts, more stressful feelings, and so on. You must free yourself from this negative spiral by breaking the chain.

How much of your day-to-day is taken up by troubling thoughts? What is the experience generally like?

_____

_____

_____

_____

What would it be like if you could live free from the torment of negative, spiraling thoughts?

_____

_____

_____

The fact is, you can't get rid of thoughts. Our minds are built to generate them. But you can let go of them.

Set a timer for three minutes. Until the timer goes off, try to write down as many troubling and worrisome thoughts as you can. Don't be shy. Let it rip!

_____

_____

_____

_____

_____

_____

_____

_____

_____

_____

_____

_____

Now tear this page out. Seriously, rip it out of the book.

Take three deep
breaths. Let the
air push way down,
stretching your
diaphragm and
relaxing all the
tension in your
abdomen.

Get rid of this page.
Burn it carefully with
a lighter or throw it
in the trash.

# That "Om" Stuff

**Used for thousands of years throughout the world,** mantra meditation—the practice of focusing your mind on a chanted word or syllable—is the most common of all meditation practices. And you can learn the basics in only a few minutes.

Before starting, you'll need to select a word or syllable as your mantra. It could be a word or sound that has personal meaning to you, or it could be nonsense. Some meditators chant a favorite color. Some use the word one. And many, of course, prefer the traditional mantra om.

Try experimenting with a few options below:

Looking back at your list, pick one that you like:

● Begin your meditation by getting into a comfortable posture. Whatever position you choose, make sure your back is straight so that the weight of your head falls directly down on your spinal column. Rock a little from side to side, and then front to back, to find a point where your upper body feels balanced on your hips.

● Now take several deep breaths. Begin chanting silently to yourself your chosen word or syllable. Just keep repeating it over and over in your mind. Or you could write it repeatedly here:

_____

_____

_____

_____

_____

_____

● You'll notice at times that your mind strays. That's fine, but always bring your focus back to the mantra.

● Now, if you're in a place where it's comfortable, try chanting the mantra aloud. Let the sound of your own voice repeating the chosen word begin to relax you. Keep focusing on and listening to the sound, over and over, monotonous yet peaceful, until you have let go of your tension.

# Seeking Your Highest Value

**In a stressful situation,** it can help to keep your eye on the one thing you most want to accomplish, the most important outcome, or the greatest disaster to avoid.

If you keep focused on your highest value, you will have won 80 percent of the battle. You might not get everything done right away, but you'll have kept up a steady pace instead of collapsing, and the goal will be in sight.

Let's use some journal space to explore your values. What kind of person would you like to be in the world? How do you want to be remembered?

What kind of parent, coworker, friend, or sibling do you hope to be?

_____

_____

_____

_____

_____

_____

How do you want to move through the world? What kind of custodian do you want to be for future generations?

_____

_____

_____

_____

_____

_____

Now pick something that has been stressful for you lately: showing up for classes on time, visiting your sick mom, paying your debts, or whatever.

In that situation, what is your highest value? What is the most important factor in coping with your stress? Resist the urge to answer, "The whole thing," or "It's all impossible." If necessary, break the task or situation down into one key part that is important and doable.

How can you tackle what might be a source of stress while pursuing what you care about at the same time?

_____

_____

_____

_____

_____

_____

_____

_____

_____

_____

See yourself handling the situation so that you preserve your highest value, no matter what. See yourself responding to your stressor with detachment and serenity.

# Looking Back from the Future

**Each separate detail of your life** is like a sticky strand of a spider web attaching you to the present. Your attention is fragmented in a thousand directions as you try to keep an eye on the kids, the mortgage, the bills, the appliances, the laundry, the grocery shopping, the cars, the boat, the lawn, the school, the job, the promotion, the raise, the spouse, the trip, the vacation, the parents, the wedding, the funeral, and so on.

Is there something you have been particularly stuck on? What is it? Why do you feel it is causing you stress?

_____

_____

_____

_____

_____

_____

_____

It seems impossible sometimes to escape the present situation, to fly out of the web and get some perspective. But you can escape from the stress of the present. Just let yourself daydream. Think about the future.

● Imagine that you are very old—still healthy and alert, but very old. You've had a long and full life. You are comfortable and secure. You are surrounded by friends and family. From this perspective, let yourself dimly remember the myriad concerns, worries, and doubts that trap you in the web of the present.

● What does this present moment look like from that vantage point?

_____

_____

_____

_____

_____

_____

● What will it all matter twenty or thirty or fifty years from now?

_____

_____

_____

● When you imagine looking back from the perspective of old age, focus on the truly important stuff that's going on in your life now. What kind of moments are available to you now that you will remember fondly in the future?

● When you return to your present point of view, try to keep your eye out for those precious moments, and let some of the minor annoyances blow away.

# Your Inner Guide

**The best way to tap into your deepest levels** of self-knowledge is to create an Inner Guide—an embodiment of your inner wisdom, an imaginary being who can clarify your feelings and help you understand yourself. Your Inner Guide can take the form of a deceased parent, a long-lost friend or teacher, a character from a novel or movie, or even a symbolic animal like an eagle or a wolf.

You can consciously decide on an Inner Guide, or you can see what kind of guide your subconscious dreams up.

- Take three deep belly breaths and relax into your body. Wait until you are in a frame of mind that allows you to conjure up a pleasant, warm, supportive, and safe guide.

- What does your Inner Guide look like? Is it someone you know? Someone you've read about or seen in a movie? Perhaps your guide is a combination of people you have known.

● What does their voice sound like?

_____

_____

_____

_____

_____

● Take a few more deep breaths and close your eyes for a moment. Ask your guide, "Are you willing to help me?" and wait for an answer. Your guide may respond with words or gestures, or you may just sense an answer or hear a voice in your head.

● What would you like them to help you with?

_____

_____

_____

_____

_____

_____

● Ask your guide, "What is causing my tension?" What kind of response do you get?

_____

_____

_____

_____

_____

● Ask, "How can I relax? What can I do to avoid stress?" What response do you get?

_____

_____

_____

_____

_____

You can consult your guide about any problems you are having, things that are worrying you, decisions you have to make, or things in your life that are unclear. You may be surprised at the simplicity and clarity of the replies. Remember that you can visit with your Inner Guide any time you need to relax or explore a problem.

# One with Nature

**Whatever the reason,** the sounds and sights of nature are inherently relaxing. That's why so many relaxation tapes feature soundtracks of waves, wind, and birdsong.

You can take advantage of this automatic association to relax yourself quickly and deeply.

One way would be to use your imagination to put yourself somewhere you've been that was naturally very relaxing. Take a moment to think, then describe what that place was:

If you have easy access to natural spaces, what are some ways you can incorporate more time in nature into your daily life?

Last, studies have shown that even representations of nature—like ocean wave sounds or pictures of trees—can improve our blood pressure and help release tension. What are some ways that you might be able to incorporate more nature—like potted plants, nature sounds, etc.—into your living and work spaces to help you relieve stress?

_____

_____

_____

_____

_____

_____

_____

_____

_____

If you're in the throes of stress overwhelm, any of these options can be the focus of a relaxation moment. Tell yourself, *I am part of nature. I live and breathe as the world lives and breathes. I can return to my natural roots anytime for refreshment and renewal.*

# Nourishment from the Past

**Your past can be a source of strength and inner calm.** It's all a matter of knowing where to look, then doing some armchair time travel to reexperience the truly nourishing moments in your life.

All you have to do is imagine four scenes from your past—using visual, auditory, and kinesthetic (touch) images.

Take a deep breath, and as you exhale, let your whole body begin to relax. Take another deep breath, and now as you exhale, allow the relaxation to deepen.

Touch your thumb to your index finger on your non-writing hand.

As the fingers touch, start to recall a time when your body felt healthy fatigue. Maybe it was after playing a strenuous sport, or digging in the garden, or hiking a steep trail. Feel how heavy and relaxed your muscles are; feel the warmth and well-being throughout your entire body. Dwell for a minute or two in the scene, enjoying the feeling. Now write the details down:

Now touch your thumb to your middle finger. As the fingers touch, go back to a time when you had a loving experience. It might be a warm embrace, an intimate conversation, or a moment of deep sexual connection. Take some time to see, hear, and feel the experience, then describe it:

Touch your thumb to your ring finger. As the fingers touch, remember one of the nicest compliments you have ever received. Hear it right now; listen carefully. Try to really let it in. What was the compliment?

_____

_____

_____

_____

_____

_____

_____

_____

Touch your thumb to your little finger. As the fingers touch, revisit the most beautiful place you have ever been. See the colors and shapes; see the quality of light. Hear the sounds of that beautiful place—the whisper of the wind through the trees or the roar of the waves. Feel that place—the texture, the warmth or coolness. Stay there for a while. Where was it?

# Anchoring

**Anchoring is a hypnotic technique** that helps you connect to times in your past when you felt truly calm and confident.

- Right now, take a slow, deep breath way down into your abdomen.

- Let your arms become heavy and relaxed. Imagine them as lead weights and feel gravity pulling them down. Your legs, too, can become heavy.

- Take another slow, deep breath, and as you exhale, feel the relaxation spread to your stomach, chest, and back. Feel your whole body letting go of the last bit of muscular tension, releasing and letting go until you are deeply, completely relaxed.

- Let a feeling of peace and calm come over you.

- Count your breaths to ten, letting the warmth and calmness grow with each breath.

- Now it's time to imagine a moment in your life when you felt something you really needed to feel right then—perhaps it was a moment when you were truly confident. Or a moment right after a success. Or a time when you felt safe and at peace. Or a situation where you felt hopeful and believed in the good times ahead.

- Go back to that moment right now. See yourself there. What were the specifics of that moment? Really drill into what was happening and how you felt.

Notice how the feeling may reflect in the way others act toward you. What do you think they saw in you?

_____

_____

_____

_____

_____

_____

_____

_____

_____

● Look inside your body now for that feeling of confidence or calm.
Find where it lives inside of you—the exact place. Experience the
confidence or calm of that moment wherever it's expressed inside of
you. Take a deep breath and, for a little while, immerse yourself in the
feeling.

● Gradually move your right hand over your left. Begin to hold your left
wrist in your right hand, gently but firmly. This gesture—your right
hand holding your left wrist—will be an anchor that can bring you
back, whenever you want, to the feeling you have right now.

Practice your anchor three or four times today until it works quickly and reliably.
You'll find it's a great tool for stress relief.

# Gratitude

**Stress creates a mental filter** that changes your reality. It's like wearing psychological dark glasses that show only your mistakes and the sad, painful things in your life.

Your life has so many things that feel good—even though there's also a lot that hurts and disappoints. You have the power to lift the mental filter by actively focusing on all the balancing realities of your life.

Take a moment for some calm, deep, and relaxed breaths.

What is one unnoticed pleasure that you experienced in the last year?

What is one satisfying thing you accomplished or experienced in the last month?

_____

_____

_____

_____

_____

_____

_____

What was one source of contentment you felt in the last week?

_____

_____

_____

_____

_____

_____

_____

This is a practice available to you whenever. We recommend that you do the following **I Am Grateful** exercise, at the end of each day, to help you affirm and remember the parts of your life that you truly value and enjoy.

● Take a slow, deep breath, and as you exhale, feel your whole body beginning to relax. Let your attention focus on three things for which you feel grateful.

● Today I am grateful for:

1. _____

2. _____

3. _____

● The three things I did today that I feel good about are:

1. _____

2. _____

3. _____

For a few moments, let yourself relive these positive events of the day.

# Treasure Chest

**Does your main stress stem from a problem you are trying to solve?**
Sometimes the best way to reduce stress is to work on solving the problem that's causing the stress.

What is the problem you are trying to solve?

_____

_____

_____

_____

_____

_____

_____

_____

_____

_____

It would be nice to have the advice of a very experienced, very wise person who knows you better than anyone else does. But where would you find such a person? Believe it or not, this wise person is you! All you have to do is ask your unconscious mind.

To solve a problem using your own inner wisdom:

● Just close your eyes for five minutes.

● Empty your mind of everything but the problem, as you breathe slower and slower and gradually relax.

● Contemplate the problem—the person, place, thing, or situation that's bothering you. Let it take center stage in your mind, but stay a little detached.

● When the problem is focused on in your mind, imagine that you are walking along a tropical beach. See the azure waves lapping the pure white sand. Feel the warmth of the sun.

● As you walk, you come to a path leading into the jungle.

● Walk up a gentle rise, under the trees. It's cooler and quieter and dimmer in here.

● Follow the path upward, following the course of a stream.

● Soon you will come to a waterfall. Walk behind the waterfall into a shallow cave. At the back of the cave, you find a small treasure chest.

● On the next page, draw what it looks like.

144

● The treasure chest contains the solution to your problem. Remind yourself of the problem by letting it enter the back of your mind.

● Kneel down and open the chest. Look at the treasure inside. There might be just one object or many things. Study the treasure you find and wonder how it might symbolize a solution to your problem.

● What did you find in the treasure chest?

● Analyzing your treasure, what does it say about how you might solve your problem?

_____

_____

_____

_____

_____

_____

_____

_____

_____

_____

● What would it look like to follow through with this insight?

_____

_____

_____

_____

_____

_____

_____

_____

_____

_____

_____

_____

_____

Do this visualization every day for a week and let the symbolic objects offered by your intuitive wisdom suggest a solution to your problem.

# Accepting Yourself

**What do you have to work with in your life?** What are your personal resources?

_____

_____

_____

_____

_____

_____

_____

_____

_____

_____

_____

_____

What are your tendencies?

What are your strengths?

What interests you?

_____

_____

_____

_____

_____

_____

_____

_____

_____

It's terribly stressful and ultimately self-defeating to go against your own grain, to try to make yourself into a totally different person than you naturally are.

That's not to say you shouldn't aspire to self-improve. It's just that you need to honestly assess your starting point and accept what you have to work with as basically okay.

The following exercise is a powerful way to quiet internal self-criticism, reestablish contact with your body in the present moment, and raise your self-esteem by simple self-acceptance.

- In a quiet moment, just close your eyes and clear your mind of all the negative, obsessive chatter that tends to go on and on. Let it get quiet inside. Let the echoes of your usual monologue die away. If a negative thought surfaces, just tell yourself, *It's only a thought*, and let it go.

- Notice how you're breathing and consciously try to slow it down. See if you can sense your own heartbeat. Listen to the sounds around you. Sense how each part of your body feels: your arms, your legs, your head, your torso.

- If you feel a pain, an itch, or a tingle, tell yourself, *That's all right. That's just how it feels right now. I can accept that.*

- As you feel more and more relaxed, make some positive, self-accepting suggestions to yourself, such as:

  - *I accept myself, whatever good or bad happens.*
  - *I can let go of the shoulds, doubts, and worries.*
  - *I'm only human; I accept my human nature.*
  - *I breathe. I feel. I do the best I can.*

Now consider it more deeply—what shoulds, doubts, and worries are *not* helping me right now?

What can I accept about myself?

What am I good at?

What do I love about myself?

What can I remember about how awesome I am, even when I am stressed out?

# • • • Stress Relief Check-In Moment • • •

Take three deep breaths and rate your stress level:

1    2    3    4    5

Where is the tension in your body?

_____

_____

_____

What might be impacting your stress levels today, negatively or positively?
Explore below:

_____

_____

_____

_____

_____

_____

How do you feel about the stress of your life? Is it high? Doable? Why did you feel that you needed this journal in this moment?

_____

_____

_____

How far away does relaxation feel at this moment in time?

_____

_____

What have you learned about either yourself or what stresses you out by working through this journal so far?

_____

_____

_____

What do you want to tell your future self the next time you feel stressed?

_____

_____

_____

**Matthew McKay, PhD,** is a professor at the Wright Institute in Berkeley, CA. He has authored and coauthored numerous books, including *The Dialectical Behavior Therapy Skills Workbook*, *Self-Esteem*, and *Couple Skills*, which have sold more than four million copies combined. He received his PhD in clinical psychology from the California School of Professional Psychology, and specializes in the cognitive behavioral treatment of anxiety and depression.

**Patrick Fanning** is a professional writer in the mental health field, and founder of a men's support group in Northern California. He has authored and coauthored twelve self-help books, including *Self-Esteem*, *Thoughts and Feelings*, *Couple Skills*, and *Mind and Emotions*.

# MORE BOOKS from
# NEW HARBINGER PUBLICATIONS

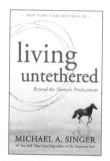

# Did you know there are **free tools** you can download for this book?

Free tools are things like **worksheets, guided meditation exercises,** and **more** that will help you get the most out of your book.

You can download free tools for this book— whether you bought or borrowed it, in any format, from any source—from the New Harbinger website. All you need is a NewHarbinger.com account. Just use the URL provided in this book to view the free tools that are available for it. Then, click on the "download" button for the free tool you want, and follow the prompts that appear to log in to your NewHarbinger.com account and download the material.

You can also save the free tools for this book to your **Free Tools Library** so you can access them again anytime, just by logging in to your account! Just look for this button on the book's free tools page.

**+ Save this to my free tools library**

If you need help accessing or downloading free tools, visit **newharbinger.com/faq** or contact us at **customerservice@newharbinger.com.**